ANIMALS
That Make a Difference!

Hummingbirds

Ashley Lee

Explore other books at:
WWW.ENGAGEBOOKS.COM

VANCOUVER, B.C.

e → WWW.ENGAGEBOOKS.COM

Hummingbirds: Pre-1
Animals That Make a Difference!
Lee, Ashley, 1995
Text © 2025 Engage Books
Design © 2025 Engage Books

Edited by: A.R. Roumanis, and Ashley Lee
Design by: Mandy Christiansen

Text set in Arial Regular.

FIRST EDITION / FIRST PRINTING

library and archives canada cataloguing in publication

Title: Hummingbirds / Ashley Lee.
Names: Lee, Ashley, author.
Description: Series statement: Animals that make a difference

Identifiers: Canadiana (print) 20230448542 | Canadiana (ebook) 20230448569
ISBN 978-1-77878-688-4 (hardcover)
ISBN 978-1-77878-697-6 (softcover)

Subjects:
LCSH: Hummingbirds—Juvenile literature.
LCSH: Human-animal relationships—Juvenile literature.

Classification: LCC QL737.P94 C38 2025 | DDC J599.885—DC23

This project has been made possible in part
by the Government of Canada.

Canada

What is that humming sound?

3

Hummingbirds are some of the smallest birds on Earth.

Hummingbirds can be many different colors.

Sometimes they look shiny.

7

Hummingbirds
have long beaks.

Sword-billed
hummingbirds have
the longest beaks.

Hummingbird wings move very fast.

They make a humming sound when flying.

Hummingbirds live in the Americas.

Most live in forests and gardens.

Hummingbirds
eat small bugs.

14

They like ants
and fruit flies.

15

Hummingbirds also drink juice from flowers.

This juice is called nectar.

Hummingbirds spread pollen between flowers.

Pollen helps plants make seeds.

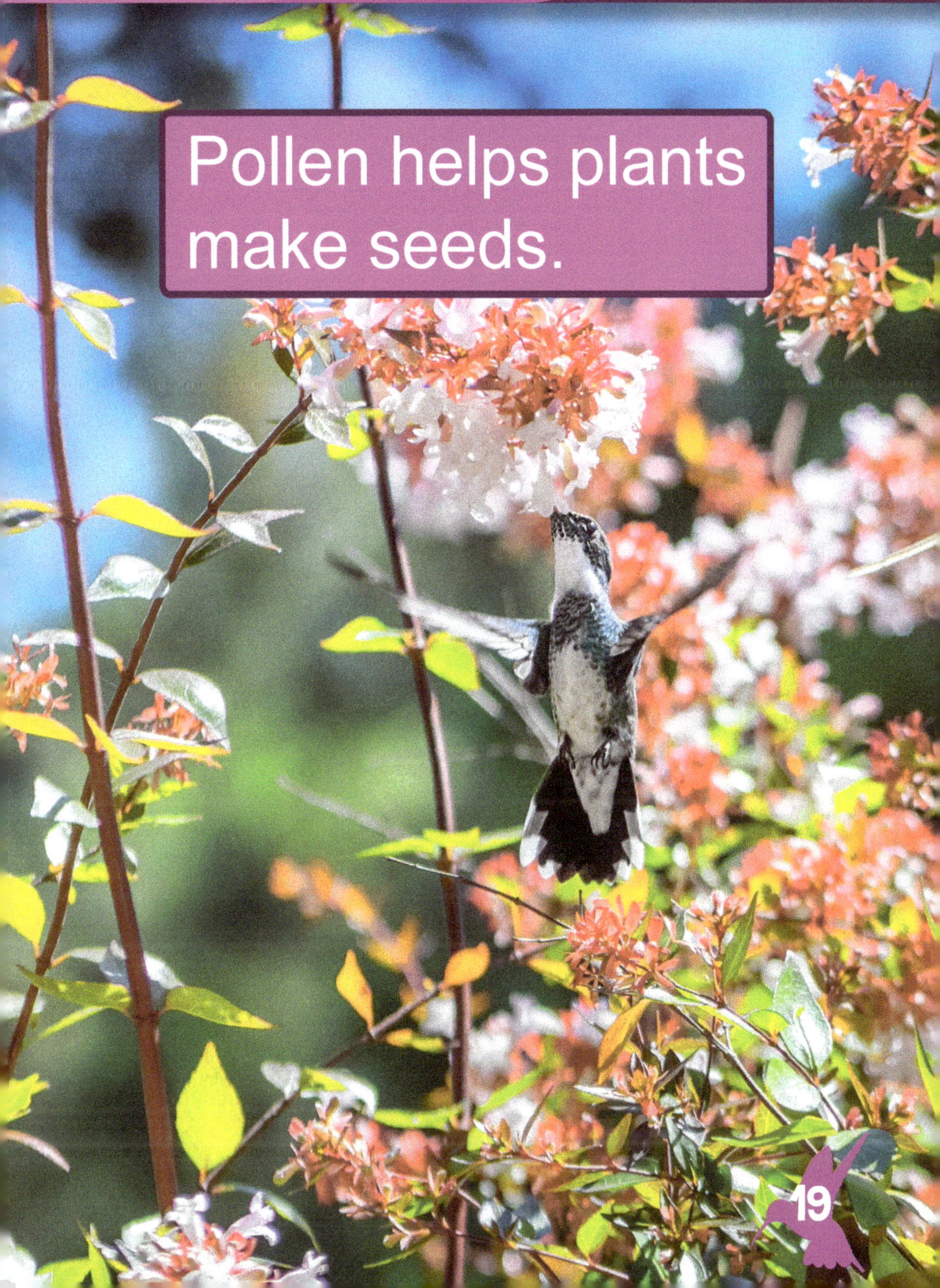

There are more plants because of hummingbirds.

21

Female hummingbirds make nests.

Nests are made of leaves, moss, and spider webs.

Hummingbirds often lay two eggs.

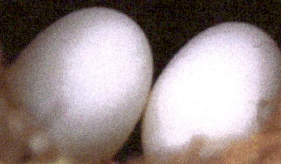

Some only have one.
Others have three.

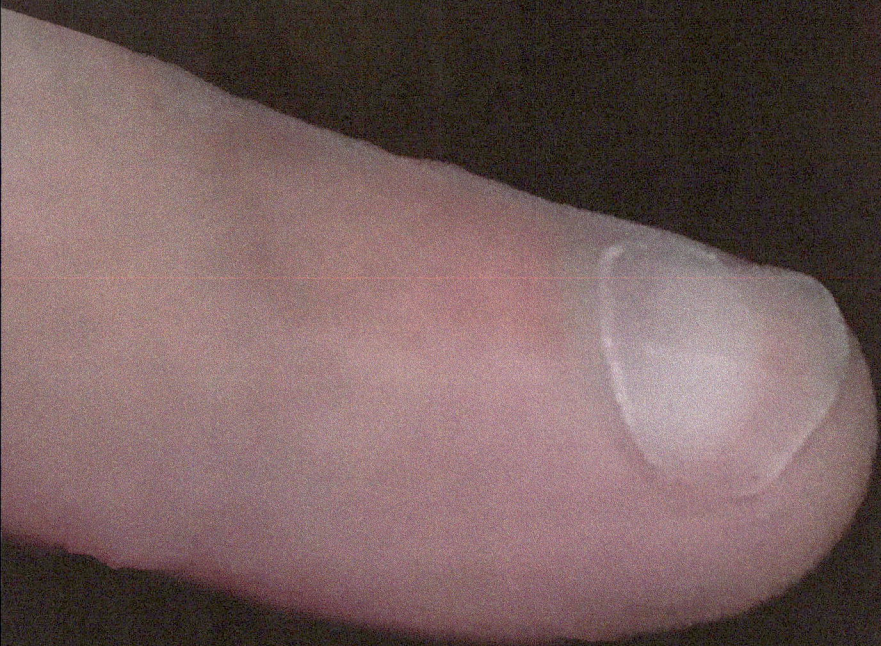

Some hummingbird eggs are as small as a pea.

Most hummingbirds live for about five years.

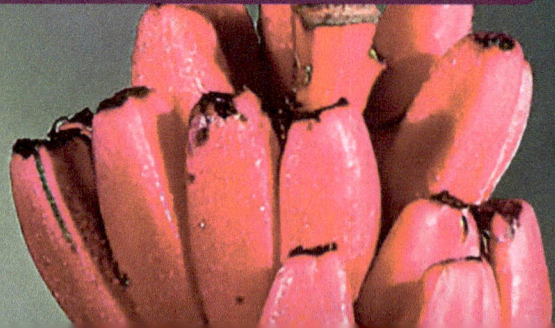

Some can live for up to 12 years.

Quiz

Test your knowledge of hummingbirds by answering the following questions. The questions are based on what you have read in this book. The answers are listed on the bottom of the next page.

1 Do hummingbirds have long beaks?

2 Do hummingbird wings move very fast?

3 Do hummingbirds eat small bugs?

4 Do hummingbirds spread pollen between flowers?

5 Are some hummingbird eggs as small as a pea?

6 Can some hummingbirds live for up to 12 years?

Explore other books in the Animals That Make a Difference series

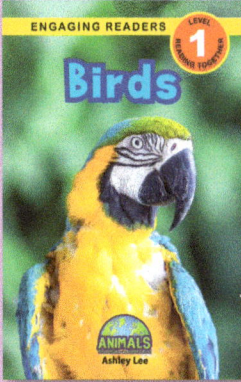

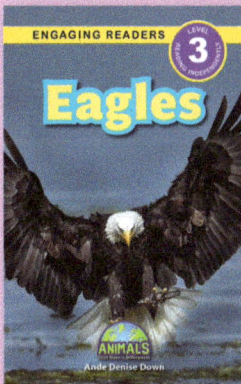

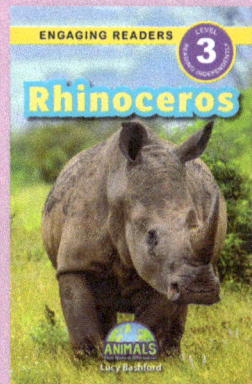

Visit www.engagebooks.com to explore more Engaging Readers.

www.ingramcontent.com/pod-product-compliance
Lightning Source LLC
Chambersburg PA
CBHW052035030426
42337CB00027B/5022